FOR MY BROTHER

CREATIVE PATTERNS

COLOURING FOR GROWN-UPS

MIA HARPER

Published by Bright Bold Publishing in 2016
First Edition, First Printing

Illustrations and cover design © 2016 Mia Harper
http://brightboldpublishing.com

ALL RIGHTS RESERVED

No part of this book may be reproduced or transmitted in any form or by any means, including but not limited to information storage and retrieval systems, electronic, mechanical, photocopy, recording, etc, without written permission from Bright Bold Publishing.

ISBN (Paperback)
978-1-911045-31-1

TO CONTACT BRIGHT BOLD PUBLISHING

Visit BrightBoldPublishing.com or send an email to Mia@BrightBoldPublishing.com

DEDICATION

Thanks mum for your support
and having faith in me

DESIGN STYLES

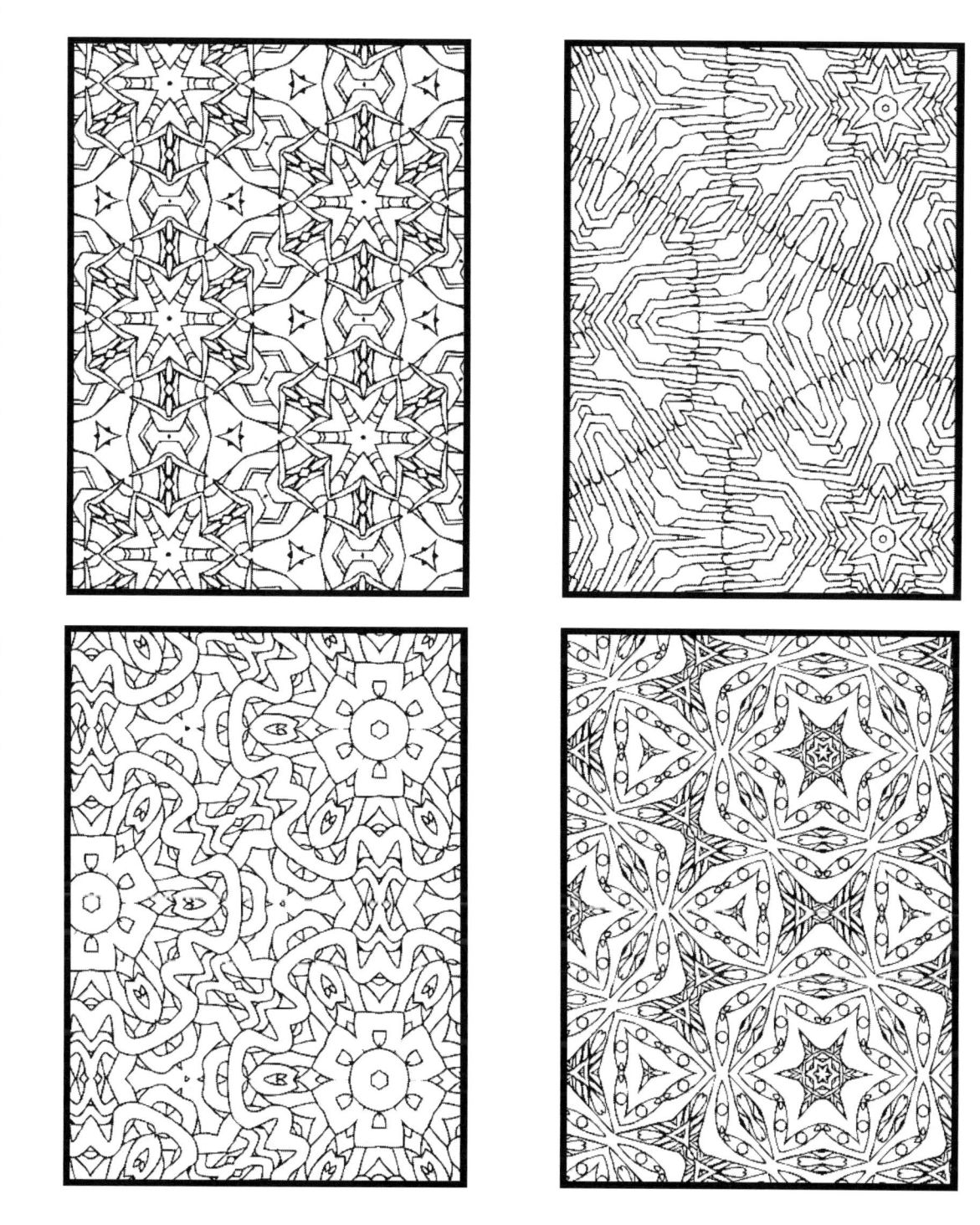

COLOUR TO CALM – BE CREATIVE

Do you find you need to switch off from the noisy world and find your own quiet corner of calm?

If this is you there's no better way than to pick up this amazing adult colouring book of 30 designs to help you escape from the day's pressures. You'll become engrossed in these patterns for meditative colouring.

The colouring book for grownups has abstract, and geometric patterns.

As you colour it'll keep you focused in the present moment and allow your creative side to emerge.

When you become absorbed in the colouring of shapes and patterns you'll unleash your creative juices and imaginative powers. You'll feel a sense of satisfaction and fulfilment at having completed a unique piece of art. Even better, over time, you'll have compiled a fantastic collection of art to be proud of, frame and decorate your walls with.

You can share this pastime with your family and friends or connect with your colouring book groups. Or, if you just want to spend some time de-stressing alone, that's okay! No drawing experience is required to create your own exceptional designs. You're free to sink into the rhythm of the shapes and lines.

For the marker enthusiasts, who love strong colours that boost your mood and uplift the soul, these designs have been created with you in mind.

You can achieve stunning results with the minimum of colours. Or if you want to walk on the 'wild' side use as many colours as you dare.

HINTS AND TIPS

Pull this book apart or photocopy the patterns onto a quality weight of paper that will work in your printer.

If you choose to colour in your book place a piece of card behind the design to avoid bleed through the paper.

Brilliant vivid markers are recommended as most of the patterns have dark lines. Strong bright colours will enhance the design.

Use Staedtler triplus fineliner, 0.3 mm - 20 Brilliant Colours for small shapes and Staedtler 20 triplus colours, 1.0 mm, for larger areas.

If you are into experimenting with colours buying a cheaper range of fibre tip pens from a supermarket in a 20 pack might do the trick. These are normally for children but you can get comparable colours though it might require you to press a little harder to get the ink flowing.

For those in the UK Sainsbury's great budget purchase of 18 pack brush markers are a good compromise. Colours are strong and vibrant and you need only apply a gentle pressure. If you press too hard you'll mash the paper fibres.

My favourite range is Djeco double ended pens. 10 per pack. You get rich hues from the felt brush and fibre tipped nibs. The ink flow is excellent. I discovered these at Hobbycraft in the UK.

Turquoise, yellow, orange, pink and bright green help highlight areas of your design.

When applying colours to larger areas of your work start with gentle fine strokes as if you were painting the surface. Go over the area again if you want to make the colour stronger. Using a light touch will help you avoid making mistakes.

Choosing colours and deciding what goes well together can be daunting. To get an appreciation of colours that work check this free website out http://www.sessions.edu/color-calculator. There are some great tutorials on colour combinations and the colour wheel.

Another way to check out colour combinations is to look at other people's artwork and model what they have done.

Mia Harper
Author/Designer

Mia lives in North West England. She is a bit of an eclectic when it comes to art.

At school she loved to illustrate her English essays and write stories. Her teacher made her cringe with embarrassment when she held up her work.

Through the help of her art teacher she was lucky enough to win a scholarship to art school and loved every moment of it.

After receiving an MA in Graphic Design she decided to move to the heady lights of London. During those early days she was flat broke and made endless pots of homemade soup.

She spent many years training other professionals in some of the top companies and advertising agencies helping them create magazines, brochures and leaflets.

When she returned to the North West she decided to stop training others and spend more time developing her own designs.

Needing to instil a manageable work life balance and address some personal issues she sought help through mindfulness therapy which set her on the road to practising living in the now.

See her unique Amazon Bestseller colouring books for grown-ups which make ideal Christmas, birthday, anniversary or Valentine's gifts for the whole family

You can find Mia at Brightboldpublishing.com and @MiaHarper007

CHECK OUT THE 'FOR MY' COLLECTION

See Mia's colouring books for grown-ups. A great gift for the wonderful person in your life. 30 Stunning patterns to colour. A great project inside for creating either a frieze or an amazing quilt to embroider. The possibilities are endless.

For My Gran
For My Mum
For My Daughter
For My Sister
For My Wife
For My Auntie
For My Niece
For My Sister-in-Law
For My Girlfriend

SEE ALL MY BOOKS OUT NOW ON AMAZON............

amzn.to/1QjksFw

Don't delay   ORDER Today

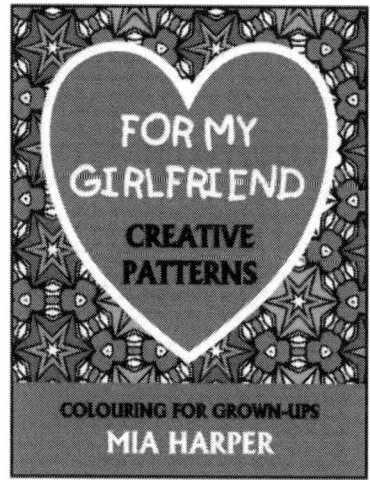

SEE THE MANDALA 'BOLD' COLLECTION

48 traditional, geometrical and abstract designs

Bold & Beautiful
Bold & Gorgeous
Bold & Distinct
Bold & Divergent
Bold & Individual
Bold & Special

CHECK OUT 'FOR MY DAUGHTER' 1 TO 5

30 Stunning patterns to colour. A great project inside for creating either a frieze or an amazing quilt to embroider. The possibilities are endless.

For My Daughter 1
For My Daughter 2
For My Daughter 3
For My Daughter 4
For My Daughter 5

Don't delay   ORDER Today

amzn.to/1QjksFw

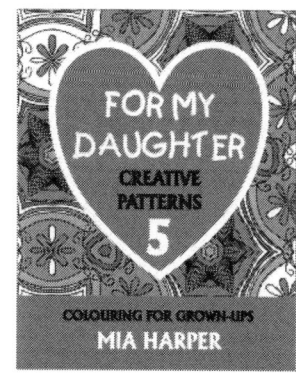

CHECK OUT 'CREATIVE MINDFULNESS' 1 TO 5

30 great abstract, geometric and floral patterns to colour with quotes to inspire you

 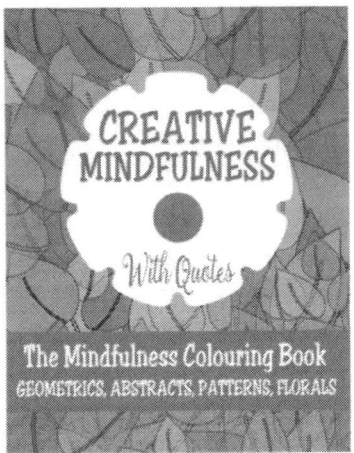

Don't delay   ORDER Today

amzn.to/1QjksFw

Thanks for buying my book and your support!

YOU'RE AMAZING

But I still need your help.
If you liked this book would you leave me
a review on Amazon?
(That would be awesome!)

Reviews are so valuable to us Indie Authors.
They help more buyers like you to find us in a
crowded market.
Only 1% of buyers ever leave a review.

If you've got two minutes, please leave a quick review.
I love featuring reviews in my books, blog and emails.
I appreciate you immensely.

Go to your Amazon account and leave a review

Printed in Great Britain
by Amazon